T0016431

PENGUIN BOOK.

Exploring Southeast Asia with Anita Magsaysay-Ho: One of Them

Eva Wong Nava is an award-winning children's book author. She writes picture books to entertain, engage, and enthral young readers. She is also an art historian. When not writing for children, she meanders art museums and galleries waiting for the next piece of art work to speak to her and inspire another story. She weaves stories from art at *CarpeArte* Journal. When not writing, Eva teaches the art of picture book creation through her workshops under the brand, Picture Book Matters. Eva can be found on Twitter, Instagram and Facebook engaging people in conversations about art and stories.

Jeffrey Say is an art historian specialising in Singapore and Southeast Asian art history. Jeffrey has been instrumental in the development of art history studies at LASALLE College of the Arts, supporting artists to develop a contextual and historical understanding of the evolution of visual arts. In 2009, he designed the world's first Master's programme focussing on Asian modern and contemporary art histories. Jeffrey is a public advocate of the importance of art history to Singapore. He is a frequent public speaker at museums, universities and galleries, and conducts short courses which remain hugely popular among various publics. Jeffrey is also a regular commentator on the local visual arts scene. An author of numerous essays on art, his seminal co- edited work *Histories, Practices, Interventions: A Reader in Singapore Contemporary Art* (2016) remains a critical anthology for researchers, curators and students on Singapore art to date.

Quek Hong Shin is a Singaporean freelance author and illustrator whose works include picture books like *The Amazing Sarong*, *The Brilliant Oil Lamp and Universe of Feelings*. *The Incredible Basket*, was the winner of Best Children's Book at the 2019 Singapore Book Awards. He is also the illustrator for other children's titles like *The One and Only Inuka* and the *Ahoy, Navy!* series that was published in celebration of the Republic of Singapore Navy's 50th Anniversary in 2017.

PENGUIN BOOKS

USA | Canada | UK | Ireland | Australia
New Zealand | India | South Africa | China | Southeast Asia

Penguin Books is part of the Penguin Random House group
of companies whose addresses can be found at global.
penguinrandomhouse.com

Published by Penguin Random House SEA Pte Ltd
9, Changi South Street 3, Level 08-01,
Singapore 486361

Penguin
Random House
SEA

First published in Penguin Books by Penguin Random House
SEA 2022

Copyright © Eva Wong Nava, Jeffrey Say, Quek Hong Shin 2022

All rights reserved

10 9 8 7 6 5 4 3 2 1

The views and opinions expressed in this book are the
author's own and the facts are as reported by her which
have been verified to the extent possible, and the publishers
are not in any way liable for the same.

ISBN 9789814954358

This book is sold subject to the condition that it shall not, by
way of trade or otherwise, be lent, resold, hired out, or
otherwise circulated without the publisher's prior consent in
any form of binding or cover other than that in which it
is published and without a similar condition including this
condition being imposed on the subsequent purchaser.

www.penguin.sg

EXPLORING SOUTHEAST ASIA WITH

ANITA MAGSAYSAY-HO

ONE OF THEM

Eva Wong Nava and Jeffrey Say

Illustrated by Quek Hong Shin

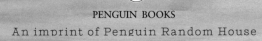

PENGUIN BOOKS

An imprint of Penguin Random House

Two female vendors are busy at work.

One is calling out 'Magandang umaga'.
'Good morning,' she says, 'come and
see what I have for you today'.

The other says 'Kumusta po'.
'Hello, look at my fresh fish,' she calls.

Anita's mouth curves into a broad smile as she listens to the sounds around her: chickens cluck, ducks quack, and women chat.

The saltiness of the sea hangs in the cool morning breeze.
The rustling of banana leaves murmurs joy across the oceans.
The familiar Filipino words are music to Anita's ears.

A woman in a
headscarf emerges.
She is carrying a
basket on her head.
A banana plant
shades her and a boy
stands nearby.

Another woman, her features plain,
is protected from the sun by a blue scarf.
She hides her shy smile behind a hand.

Here is one bent at her waist.
She is hauling fishing nets with a group of women.

I like to see my women working.

*Sometimes, I paint them standing prettily with
flowers... but I like to see them more at work.*

Anita's women are from the Zambales province in the Philippines. She spent many summer months there playing, observing, and connecting with these strong, hardy peasant women when growing up.

10

Anita infused her painterly lines and shapes with vigour and energy.

She transcribed her happy memories of childhood on canvas.

Anita travelled around the world, and she continued to be fascinated by the many markets she had visited.

Disaster struck when Anita was twenty-eight years old.
The Second World War began and her idyllic days at
Zambales soon became pipe dreams.
Like everyone in Southeast
Asia, Anita and her family lived
in fear and dread under the
Japanese occupation.

The people of the Philippines were brought to their knees. They prayed and prayed for almost four years before the Japanese forces were defeated.

Anita shuts her eyes. The eastern Pacific winds meet the breezes from the West Philippine Sea lulling her to sleep. She dreams of Luzon Island and of the many women from the Zambales province who have filled her life with joy and inspiration.

Her love for them would move her to capture their graceful and humble bodies at work and in motion.

I know very well the strength, hard work and quiet dignity of Philippine women, for I am one of them.

25